The Sustain Pedal

The Sustain Pedal

Poems by Carol Jennings

Cherry Grove Collections

Published by Cherry Grove Collections
P.O. Box 541106
Cincinnati, OH 45254-1106

ISBN: 9781625494009

Poetry Editor: Kevin Walzer
Business Editor: Lori Jareo

Visit us on the web at www.cherry-grove.com

Cover photograph by Joseph Llobrera

Acknowledgments

With gratitude to the editors of the journals where some of the poems in this collection have previously appeared:

Chautauqua: "Moulin"

Beltway Poetry Quarterly:

> "The Viscosity of Corona Time"

> "Playing Brahms' Intermezzo in A Major"

> "Chopin in Exile"

Loch Raven Review: "Beethoven, Piano Concerto No. 1"

Gargoyle Magazine:

> "*Fur* Beethoven from Elise"

> "A New York Summer: West 14th Street"

> "Meditation on Feet"

That you are here—that life exists and identity,
That the powerful play goes on, and you may
contribute a verse.

Walt Whitman, "O Me! O Life!" *Leaves of Grass*

for Luka and Marina

Table of Contents

I. An Unyielding Sense of Time

II. Intermezzo

III. The Layered Life

I. An Unyielding Sense of Time

A Flickering Light

Why so much time
before I grasped
its place in my life?
Before I understood
the possibility
to bend and stretch,
fold it into poems,
stories, save it
for dark seasons,
follow it north or south,
depending upon month
and hemisphere, or
simply keep it in some
mind pocket until
needed to deflect
the dark.
As a child in thrall
to midsummer light,
enough to bicycle
home at nine o'clock,
with no thought about
the slant of it to come
as days shorten and insects
grow frantic and shrill
about sex and death,
I thought I could use it

all up, the euphoria,
reserve nothing for later.
Now I have mastered
the art, or perhaps trick,
of parsing it out
in lesser portions
to make it last,
the way a flickering light
can trick the eye to see it
as a constant, and knowing
this may be the antidote
to everything.

Beethoven's Ode to Joy

You begin with tentative notes,
emerging soft from silence —
this at a time you live in silence,
creating sound only from memory.
Strings struggle with A and E,
cascade in broken fourths and fifths,
before settling in key of D minor.
Fragments connect, development
never resolves into recapitulation,
then at last an undulating coda.
The Scherzo teases repetition, but
changes course, offers a drum.
Serene adagio hints at melody to come
until trumpet and drum intrude,
predict something not heard before.

A melody the mind can clutch,
hum along, even with no
sound or score. Perhaps first
a flash in your youth, it evolved
over decades in your messy sketch
books — first a little love song, then
variations for the Choral Fantasy,
finally coming close in your tribute
to King Stephen of Hungary.

It is ready for the last symphony,
but you hold off to the end, prepare
your audience to be overwhelmed
as if falling in love the first time.

You give space, tonality, rhythm
to review an entire life,
even the life of our species,
until dissonant triads interrupt
and finally human voices stretch
composer boundaries to build almost
a symphony within a symphony.
Your last song now comes into itself.
You borrow words from Schiller,
but remove all lines about
drink and drunkenness
as joy can never be induced.
You wrote for the future,
a grander orchestra
in another century—
like the Berlin concert
for a wall torn down
when Bernstein changed
joy to *freedom*,
certain of your approval.

Between Unknown and Unknowable

the chemical elements of love

insides of a black hole

duration of our species

if death spins a vision

whether any god or the soul is real

how Beethoven navigated the 5th
      from knock of hard fate in broken C-minor chord
      to celebration in C major cadence,
      while also growing deaf in a city under siege

how Mahler twice breached the distance
      from simple melody of insecurity
      to cosmic choral ecstasy

if Brahms and Clara consummated love
      with more than a look or touch

what was in grandmother's mind when she held
      a knife to her throat just before Christmas

whether the creatures of my dreams have teeth

all of these I wish to be unknowable because with age
      mystery gives rise to apparitions
      more seductive than the knowing.

Poem Beginning with a Line of Rainer Maria Rilke

Every angel is terrifying
until you reach a certain time
when they begin to appear
in the half-awake dreams
of pre-dawn sleep,
especially in early summer
while cicadas vibrate a song
saved underground for 17 years.
They remind you not only of loss,
but of what you will do that day,
pick strawberries for breakfast,
sweep spent wings from the porch,
invite a spirit companion to share
your strawberries and describe
the possibility of another life,
a before or after life,
with a different tonality
and absence of rhyme.

After a Certain Age

Do not count the number
of funerals attended,
people who have professed
to love you, foreign
countries not visited,
vanishing rings of Saturn,
wrong notes played
in a Mozart sonata, or
inches of sea level rise.
And do not listen to
the noise that is news
nor the harsh words
of the Dies Irae.
You will know when
you have reached
that age.
Pay attention
to stars in the darkest skies,
planets visible to your unaided eye,
lengthening daylight
after winter solstice,
layers of igneous rock
in deep canyons,
your ancestors,
time as an artificial construction,
music that outlives its composer.

Unfinished

I moved to New York at 20 to let go
of things too familiar: streets named
for deciduous trees and an evergreen;
family who thought they knew me;
the melancholy of a room bound
in flowered wallpaper; love
for a physicist in love with
sub-atomic particles.

                    *

A young Michelangelo carved
Madonna of the Steps—Mary,
with such large hands, deep folds
in her garment, nursing her son.
He died at 88 leaving an unfinished
fourth *Pieta*, Mary holding upright
the body of her slain son, as if
she might will life back into him.

                    *

When is the moment to let go?—
your clasp of a child's hand,
dead lover who invades dreams,
G major last chord with a long hold,
grasping the origin of the universe,
fear of a very dark angel.

Calving

Greenland glaciers calve
with sonorous ring,
while ablation of ice mass
turns blue meltwater rivulets
into quiet rivers to the sea.

I fell in love with glaciers
because their language is rich
with French; and also feared them
because my earth science text
warned another ice age could come,
though not quickly.

I made a list of things to do:
walk then kneel on a glacier top,
drink the waters of a moulin,
see the Matterhorn, read tales
of hikers falling in a crevasse,
listen to the harmonies of calving.

Now I have done all of these,
and no longer fear the ice,
but the loss of it; glaciers,
sentries that warn of ancient microbes,
the warm human finger-print, the tipping point,
Greenland waters at the door.

Moulin

After Seamus Heaney

Take the time to walk back to the Pleistocene.
Just off the highway between Jasper and Banff,
park the car to board a snow bus that deposits
you on the ice field, where you can guzzle
glacial meltwater from a moulin — water
with the purity that preceded your species.
Pay attention, or you could tumble into
a crevasse from which you would not emerge
until the ice has melted. Kneel down, touch
the glacial tongue with reverence. But know
that you violate it. Consider that it recedes
and loses depth beneath your body, that
it may disappear within the life of your child.
Let the ice pierce a hole in you even as it melts.

All Hallows' Eve

Where are the songs of Spring? Ay, where are they?
Think not of them, thou hast thy music too,—
John Keats, "To Autumn"

Because of tilt of earth and angle
of sunlight, autumn crisps and curls
across summer's fading fullness
in its unrelenting passage.

This is a time with its own colors—
gold, maroon, and burnt red—
in a leaf patchwork that floats
after the heavy downpour,

more flamboyant on water
than waving on branches in air.
Summer insect whine is silenced
by death or sleep. The bird's nest

abandoned for another hemisphere.
Music replaced by acorns falling
and burrowing creatures that crunch
their way through downed leaves.

Such a brittle time.
The thin line between living
and dead blurs. A spirit slips
easily between worlds.

We live on a slant, and light travels
the shortest path through the sky.

At Winter Solstice

This is the time to attend to the dark:
candles burned to a pool of wax,
Christmas lights dimmed. News
that is not good—Greenland melts,
rainforests fall, New South Wales on fire.
Even as earth heats up, my body
chills down to stiff fingertips. Time
runs short for tasks done best in natural light—
playing Liszt scores, with notes for right hand
jammed between notes for the left, or
reading Hawking on curvature of space and time.
Hawking, whose mind expanded like the universe
he probed until his body became cosmic dust.
He posed a new possibility—*that space and time*
together might form a finite, four-dimensional
space without singularities or boundaries.
This fourth dimension I try to absorb as I count
daily the added minutes and seconds of sunlight,
and look into the dark eyes of newborn Marina,
pushed early into the universe. They flicker
bits of blue like the dark deep of oceans.

Pantoum for Pele

Pele's spirit lingers in the caldera
goddess of fire killed by her sister
remains of her body are hot magma
lava fountains she spews when angry

goddess of fire killed by her sister
Pele formed these islands from
lava fountains she spews when angry
after plates move and mantle plume rises

Pele formed these islands from
explosions of lava, black sand, seawater
after plates move and mantle plume rises
Hawaiians accept her volatility

explosions of lava, black sand, seawater
wound into this chain of fertile islands
Hawaiians accept her volatility
eruptions the price of Pele's gifts

wound into this chain of fertile islands
tips of the world's longest mountain range
eruptions the price of Pele's gifts
of cliffs, sand beaches, warm waves

tips of the world's longest mountain range
cooling lava leaves behind an island
of cliffs, sand beaches, warm waves
little paradise that begins to sink

cooling lava leaves behind an island
and Pele will take back her land
little paradise that begins to sink
as she prepares to surface again

and Pele will take back her land
her spirit lingers in the caldera
as she prepares to surface again
remains of her body still hot magma

Snow in May

For Nancy

You would like that it fell on the day
we buried you on a hillside in Vermont.

You would joke that we forgot our skis,
how the weather was perfect for the occasion.

We had little to say aloud, but wrote messages
on slips of paper to place in the cherry wood box.

Those letters among the ashes still connect us
to you, knowing how much you would love

the snowflakes clumping on apple blossoms,
as out of harmony as your early death.

Australia Travel Guide

This country warns
of so many ways to die—
box jellyfish, bluebottle, stingray,
blue-ringed octopus, cone shell,
stonefish, lionfish,
saltwater crocodile,
taipan and tiger snake,
red-back and funnel web spider,
razor-clawed cassowary.

Yet it seduces you
with sands of silk,
holy red rock,
Ulysses butterflies,
rainforest basket ferns,
fairy penguins,
blue-winged kookaburra,
figs strangling raintrees,
white blooms that last
a night, fall in the river
with morning.

Corals secrete their habitat,
the living build upon the dead
to form ocean canyons
red, pink, yellow, purple.
You will swim among them
to mourn that earth
is killing them with heat.

This lonely continent
without borders
will overwhelm.
You can't absorb enough,
but want to know it all—
even the hot emptiness,

unforgiving desert,
a topography that kills
if you stray too far alone.
In spite of the dangers,
you won't want to leave
because you will fall
in love with this under-
belly of the planet,
where the sun on eucalypts
glazes mountains blue.

The Canyon We Call Grand

Here, as nowhere else,
earth exposes herself—
scars of stress
in layer upon hard layer of
granite, gneiss, schist,
Redwall Limestone,
Bright Angel Shale.

When tectonic plates collided,
the lighter continental
mounted the heavier oceanic,
an act of force geologists call
subduction.

Through hot years of pressure,
rocks rose, did not collapse,
folded, did not break.
Monsoon rains pummeled,
and rivers cut a deep divide.

They come from all continents,
voyeurs of a planet unclad,
history of wounds in her strata.
Parents grasp children's
sunburned hands, peer down
into this abyss of violent time.

The Viscosity of Corona Time

The days become
slow moving water.
The mirror blurs
your face while
your mind can
barely skim
the surface
of anything.
Quarantine causes
headache,
imbalance,
numb spirit,
flattened affect,
symptoms
seldom fatal.
And a glass of wine
may enhance
perception of
blended time.

Things change only in sleep
when you can walk close
to others, even touch
a stranger. In dreams,
the rules change—
there are no masks,

all intruders are visible.
Though the virus may
helicopter around you,
even light on your
hair or an eyelash,
it has not mutated to
invade the subconscious
of REM sleep.

In my childhood,
they warned against
swimming in the creek
because polio might lurk
in the water, waiting
to kill or cripple children.
But we did not wear
masks, and we could touch
almost anything.

Mother liked to tell
how she nearly died
in the 1918 epidemic.
In old age, she remained
angry at the doctor
who delivered
a grim prognosis
in deep voice
at the door of her room.

Father was a pharmacist
who instructed me about
proper hand washing,
cough covering,
germs that linger
invisible in the air,
flit person to person,
enter the body
like an evil spirit.
If he were alive,
he would work
through this epidemic,
count pills,
measure liquids,
mix compounds,
gloved and masked,
tell me too often
that he was right.

Ultima Thule

On the icy fringes
of a solar system we call ours,
your two spheres melded
in soft collision. Bright scarf
circles the point of contact
so you resemble a lopsided
snowman, look not unfriendly
as caught in photos by
spacecraft hurtling to reach
outer edge of the Kuiper Belt
before burning out.

I look at three-quarters of a century,
measured in revolutions
around the sun, a few lines
written, adagios on the piano,
ancient ruins entered, dreams
that twist dark reality,
the deaths that keep coming.
On Mauna Kea, the Milky Way
seems to wrap itself around
our lonesome minor planet, where
I have never felt at home.

Ultima Thule, you will be
among the last to melt
as our star expands in death throes.
Your name meaning
place beyond the known—
I want it to be yours alone.

Clairvoyance

At age six, glasses became part of my face
     so I could see the elegance of numbers,
     one added to another with chalk

then I came to hate them

for their weight, interruption of a self-image,
     distance imposed between me and what I saw

years later I traded them for plastic circles
     I could drop in an eye with one finger

to look far down a New York Street
     discern the pale green of new leaves curling softly
               against gray limbs

recognize faces that approach

read a lover's expression and feel a world close to me again
     as in the early years with new eyes

I also turned my sight inward on curves of fear and
               concentric circles of solitude

I don't mind a slight blur after standing at a canyon's edge
      to count rock strata that reveal the brevity of my time

to look across an unpolluted night sky that proves
      the slight measure of my place in the dust

Vertigo

Let faces from the past whirl
on the crown molding of your room
to ask you why.
Let your childhood friends blindfold you,
twirl you around, make you beg them to stop.
Please let there be a potion, powder or brew to drink,
a chant, incantation or rhyme that twists on the tongue
to make things right again.
Please let all creatures with legs be balanced.
You can only lie flat, eyes fixed straight ahead
as the carousel spins around you
taunting with its brassy sound.
This repeats daily until

the dizziness is done. Then
you descend stairs,
rip off the blindfold,
draw perfect sixteenth notes on parchment,
play them in your head or on ivory keys,
listen to the sound waves of the brain,
read your fortune in tea leaves,
taste the bitter cube of the body's fragility,
and swallow it.

Blue

Blues on a brush jar that holds my pens—cobalt, lapis, azure,
and pale blue make a blue jagged mountain, blue tree rooted
in a blue mound by a small house outlined in blue, with a distant
blue sail on water and a few birds blue in flight. There is a blue
for each phase of a mood that travels from dark to light and
back again.

*

The Dutch named Delft blue for a city where potters tin glazed
a cheaper version of Chinese porcelain. Vermeer painted blue
scarves and dresses on Delft women and girls. My friend Helen,
who chose to be Dutch, could have stepped out of a Vermeer
portrait in her blue skirt and matching scarf and a mood more
sun yellow than any shade of blue. He might have painted her
as she talked to yellow birds and tabby cats at the same time.
In her presence, they were friends.

*

Years before Delft, I visited Beijing and walked Liulichang, street named for kilns that fired glazed tiles for Ming temples and palaces. I was eager to buy calligraphy on scrolls, stone rubbings on rice paper, teacups, brush jars. I was a foreigner in my own body, and in this ancient country where I knew no words and understood nothing.

Year of My Birth

Nazis had infested most of Europe.
An amphibious force of liberators
landed on French beaches
just before summer solstice.
The mission would take a year.

In August, a girl of 15 was taken
from an Amsterdam attic, sent
by train to Westerbork, Auschwitz,
Bergen-Belsun, always ahead of
Allied advance. She did not reach 16.

The City of Light was entered
by American soldiers amidst
cheers, outstretched hands and
kisses. Parisians gave them bread.
They gave Parisians rides in jeeps.

Bing Crosby crooned a question—
Would you like to swing on a star?
Lead Belly sang goodnight
to Irene, a suicide wish
buried in his second verse.

Leonard Bernstein conducted his first
symphony, borrowing from Jeremiah's
prophesy and lament for Hebrew
suffering—a chorus with no words
of hope or redemption.

I crawled under the grand piano,
where Mother played her homage
to a more romantic time,
watched her right foot depress
then release the sustain pedal
again and again.

II. Intermezzo

Fugue and Counterpoint

At the piano, I am grateful
to those medieval monks
who did not abandon
the monastery and
developed the note system
in which I find solace
playing irreverent Mozart
and Lutheran Bach
who invented complex forms,
fugue and counterpoint,
yet still believed that
sheep may safely graze
even in the dark.

Conversation with Beethoven

He glowers as he often did before.
I wonder if this will be possible—
he was deaf, I don't speak German.
Does language still matter? I ask.
He shakes his head. This was to be

your year—250th birthday celebration.
He half smiles. Every orchestra
programmed you—all
the symphonies and concertos,
Missa Solemnis, *Fidelio*, quartets.
But a novel virus seized
the living world—everything
had to be canceled. He shrugs
as though he knows or perhaps
doesn't care much. Do you
pay attention to performances
anymore? He shakes his head.
I'm guessing you like the size
of orchestras now—it's what
you always wanted isn't it?
Again, he almost smiles.
I am suddenly aware of music,
unlike any I have heard before.
What is that, where is it coming from?
It's not like anything you ever wrote.

Finally he smiles, motions me closer,
speaks in a language I do not know
but understand:
I am no longer bound
by a system of tones
that can be sketched on paper—
I am truly free.

To Michelangelo's Dying Slave

No pain mars your marble face,
your pose almost erotic, left arm
flung back behind your head,
right hand fingering the spear
slit in your chest, one knee bent,
your David-like face tilted
slightly away from us, eyes
shut. Your vision inward,
release on your face
as you die at your peak.

Your body still radiates
desire, like a new star,
even as you enter that space
beyond desire—
as if you hear a melody
like the *Liebestod*,
composed 300 years after
your dying was carved,
that one-time song
when love and death
meld before the end.
If you could speak,
you would tell us
nothing.

Playing Brahms' Intermezzo in A Major

Intermezzo, an arc, an interlude,
connects pieces of a story or dance,
but for you, it became the whole,
not the bridge between.

The *motif* here is longing,
one too pure for language,
even that of poetry,
too pure to touch.

I play the A Major to link
you and Clara, the golden haired
young composer and the dazzling
pianist with eyes of deep lapis

and a mad, music-genius husband.
I practice each day to work your
longing into my fingers on the keys,
knowing the music will never resolve.

It began when you knocked
on the Schumann door in Dusseldorf.
In their parlor you played the piano,
first with an echo of Beethoven,

then your own contrapuntal inventions,
polyphonic fabric, shifting accents.
You paused as Robert summoned Clara,
and out of her electric gaze,

the arc ascended. Part of a skewed
triangle, you loved her, but devoted yourself
to him, through his one-way descent
into the black tunnel of his mind.

Even when Clara was widowed,
you could not marry her—
perhaps because you felt stained
by the women and men

at the dockside Hamburg brothel—
where the blonde boy of you
once played a tinny piano
for coins to feed your family.

You could never make love
to one you actually loved,
or love one with whom
you shared a bed.

The longing made its own life—
not the entr'acte, but the act itself—
connected to no ending but death,
whichever death came first.

Pompeii

I listen for the voices of trapped spirits,
and hear you whisper in stone shadows:
I was so young, so alone that day.

Not knowing your name, I call you
Olivia, to honor these olive groves
where you walked hot afternoons.

At the natatorium, I see your body —
smooth and lithe slithering
into the waters on still mornings.

I felt the earth tremble as it did
once when I was a child,
and that time we lived.

I want to know more of you,
what you wore, what you thought
that morning as you scanned the sky,

observed the plume described by Pliny
as an umbrella pine —
as though it might shelter against the deluge.

And not knowing, I have to paint your life—
you in a white garment, blue stones
around your neck and wrist, served

by a young slave, who desired you.
Did you turn to him when your husband
traveled to sell his wine or olive oil?

Yes, but that day I was alone,
here where I like to hover now
with the frescoes of lovemaking,

where lapis blues, ferrous reds
and oranges survived though life did not,
as we choked on the poison of Vesuvius.

I want to tell you how we know
where people lay in death,
the positions of bodies in those final

moments, before they were molded
by the pumice and ash that rained
down, hardened around them.

But we move on to the market square,
while your spirit remains in shadows.
Olivia, you are still felt here—

a gossamer presence among the throngs,
tourists that traipse through ruins,
feeling lucky not to have been in the path.

And I have given you a voice, ruffled
your uneasy rest, exposed your secrets,
tried to bring you out of the ruins.

The volcano has not finished with us,
but next time we may have more warning.
When it erupts, perhaps you can drift

above it all, examine the plume
from its other side—
finally escape its shadow.

Beethoven, Piano Concerto No. 1

In a chill Vienna rain,
a dash to the Konzerthaus
for your first piano concerto—
actually the second in time—
composed as a century closed
and you first knew your ears
were failing you. I wonder
how you dealt with cold and damp
in your fingers as you worked out
solo parts on the keys—
or perhaps you didn't feel it at all
as the inner voice propelled its way
out of you. By the Largo in the middle,
I am warmed, emboldened, believe
perhaps I can play this too.

A year later, it is winter, and
as afternoons darken—
earlier each day—I open
my mother's ragged score to that page
where your melodic yearning
will overheat me once again.
This is lonely work—
parsing only solo passages,
pausing for long measures
given only to strings or winds

that I have to play in my head,
as you did too,
alone in your upstairs flat.

This is how I connect myself
to a century that is not mine,
to buried family, to dreams
of a space I cannot visit.
Just absorbing the notes,
getting the touch and tempo,
the muted desire almost right
will suffice.

Russian Dream

I dream myself
in St. Petersburg,
a city I have never seen.
The time is fifty years
before I am born,
and the *Pathétique* is débuted,
led by the composer
just nine days before
his mystery death.
I am pulled into the lyric
of dolorous descent
in his second theme,
as I have been every time,
since I heard it
first at age ten.
When the end comes,
and the pulsating cellos
fade into stillness,
I want to tell him—
before I am forced
to leave the dream
for my own life—
that I know
he was not free to love,
and I am sorry.

It Is Mid-Winter in the Ural Mountains as Lara and Zhivago Part for the Last Time—She in a Horse-Drawn Sleigh Driven by a Man She Once Shot

Mother's music box played Lara's theme
when she raised the lid. She did not know
the story, and I would not tell her that
Lara was the other woman for Zhivago.
Always, it is the other woman shrouded by
the lyrical love theme, the wistful melody
that makes you want for her to have
what she wants, that makes you wish,
almost, to be her. That conversation
I could not have with my mother.

Though she might have given in to
a few tears when Lara leaves the dacha
by sleigh protected only by the older man
who raped her as a teen and whom she shot
with poor aim in response. She confesses
she is pregnant by the poet, and you know
it is over for them. In real life, it was worse;
Pasternak's lover may have betrayed him
to the KGB. This is where the love theme
tells only half the story, or less.

Chopin in Exile

Polish mother, French father,
you adopted the French form
of Frédéric, became Parisian
though always homesick
for Warsaw, seized by Russia
while you played piano in Vienna.
Never to return home again
in your too-short life,
you poured yourself into
a poetry of tones with
Polish rhythms—mazurkas,
accent on second beat, polonaises,
accent on second half of first beat,
harmonic questions,
dissonance slow to resolve,
a music of fleeting emotion,
passion mixed with ambiguity
like your uneasy love for the novelist,
Aurore, who preferred to be called
George, wore trousers, smoked cigars,
took lovers, and cared for you
as consumptive coughing
wasted your body. Unlike other
composers of your time,
you eschewed the romance
of fanciful titles or story lines

and would be disturbed to know
that in the centuries after yours
you have scored films with
titles like The Innocent,
The Spy Who Loved Me,
Spiral Staircase,
The Death of Stalin,
Bodily Harm. Movies
that could have made you
wealthy, though never happy.

What would please you today
is that you still speak to Poland
and to pianists, in places
you never knew, who gather
to share interpretations
of nocturnes, waltzes, études,
ballades, impromptus, and
to speak of love for you.

Fur Beethoven from Elise

You ruined me for other men,
you know. I have been loved
by others more handsome than you,
with gentle touch and pretty words.
But each time I begin to fall,
your teasing eighth notes
that presage the melody
course through me to intervene.

It was a trifle for you, your A minor
Bagatelle with its little arcs and bridges
always coming back to that winsome lyric—
forever implanted in my body and brain—
a theme that never fully resolves,
like my feelings for you.

Your publisher got my name wrong
(due to your terrible handwriting).
Elise does not exist,
though she will outlive me
to taunt generations of piano students
who will love or hate her for
testing them, making fun of their
imperfect playing—
much as you did to me.

I could never possess you or you me,
yet because of that little piece—
dashed off in an hour, no doubt—
we will stay forever linked,
what we both wanted, I believe.

Sylvia at the Edge

Here once before
in the yew's shadow,
she should not have
returned to try again.

The fever is down,
kitchen floor is cold.
Doors are sealed,
milk has been poured.

Poems float on mail boat
to New York. Nursemaid
will come soon enough.
Nothing more to arrange.

The body will be perfected,
the moon will not be sad.
Too cold for any fly to buzz,
just a slight hiss of gas.

Her yew is black, silent,
ready to purify the dead.

What Roth Gave Us

A patient on the analyst's couch tries to overcome his Jewish
mother, taking three *shiksa* lovers nicknamed The Monkey,
The Pumpkin, The Pilgrim. A ghost of Anne Frank inhabits
two novels about an alter ego. History is altered when
Lindbergh is elected president and favors Hitler. Daughter
of a glove-maker bombs a village post office to protest Vietnam.
A professor who redefined his race is accused of racial slur.
And a professor with a breast fixation wakes to find himself
metamorphosed into one. A puppeteer performs carnal acts in
graveyards, while thinking of suicide. Roth's last word revisits
the poliovirus.

*

Polio fear permeated your early years. You climbed down
creek banks, but did not jump in because the virus might lurk
in the waters. You read history, especially stories of women
who changed it. Anne was imprinted on your conscience
because she was taken by Gestapo the same year you were born.
Teachers forgot to mention that Lindbergh was an anti-Semite.
You adopted politics opposite those of parents, aunts, uncles,
but blowing up anything seldom occurred to you. Fiction made
you wiser—first Salinger and Michener, later Dostoyevsky and
Roth. Sex described in words shocked you, but only for a little
while. You decided to be a *shiksa* to a Jewish lover.

*

Now we are vaccinated against the old viruses, while new ones
evolve. We swim freely in waters that will either dry up or
overtake us. There is no more hiding under our desks to prepare
for nuclear attack. We adjust to new danger—in the fates of
Antarctica, Amazon rainforest, burning lands. The universe is
expanding. Extinction is a possibility. And Roth is gone.
The plot against America spreads again, but he cannot write a
solution. The human stain widens in concentric circles as he
warned. Buried at Bard, he is out of reach of critics, his characters
free to re-invent themselves, twist plots, change endings—
what we all wish for.

Piano Lesson

First I learned to read words.
Next my mother taught me
to read notes in a score
by counting lines and spaces.

It was the late 1940s.
War had ended.
The town relaxed.
My small mind
brimmed over with
its ability to decode
both words and notes.

Sharps and flats followed,
the thrill of reaching up
to press an ebony black key,
of finding the right note
without looking down.

Beginner books bored me,
though I was drawn
to some of the titles—
Swans on the Lake and
The Scissors Grinder.
My town had neither.

I knew I could never match
the alacrity of mother's
long fingers on the keys.
She told me to keep trying.

There was a year
of practicing
To a Wild Rose
for a teacher who
always criticized.
I gave up on both.

Another year, my rendition
of *Slaughter on Tenth Avenue,*
with jazz rhythms
and *forté* glissando,
triggered loud applause
at a student recital
in a dank auditorium.
I decided no more recitals.
I could not top *Slaughter.*

At sixteen, I fell in love
with at least two boys
and Chopin's Nocturne in E flat,
popularized as a movie song
called *To Love Again.*
The boys disappeared.

I believed Chopin
would not mind
if I made his nocturne
a theme for my disquiet.

Portrait in Tones of Gray

The eyes betray you, lady,
long hair drawn back,
face composed too tight,
you smile too easily, yet
behind those blue-gray eyes,
you knew your husband
would leave one day, you knew
your children were borrowed —
you belong to nothing
and nothing belongs to you.
Cats do not like you, lady,
they will not lick your hand
with love. You lament too softly,
lady, men have died of you —
you who do not believe
in weddings, funerals,
or public expression
of private sorrow,
you hold nothing sacred —
in your room no lover,
you have rejected
every comfort,
no book, no flower
by your side,
you are too alone,
lady.

Meditation: Spring, Mendelssohn, Songs Without Words

It was never just about lengthening light,
the sun shifting hemispheres,
buds that presage blossoms,
or my being born,

there was always a darker side.

And then death happened,
father at equinox, mother a few days before.
Spring became about endings too.

Whatever the season, or infection circling the world,
I return to Mendelssohn's *Lieder ohne Worte*,
                              songs without words for piano,
and try to bar from my conscious self any language but tones.

These songs are not about anything.

                              *

At nine, Mendelssohn set Psalm 19 to music:
      The heavens declare the glory of God, and the firmament
                                showeth his handiwork.
Later he decided words were too limiting.
Poems could be built solely with tones.

In the Hebrides, he created a landscape
                      without words or paint,
calling it first *The Lonely Island.*
Open fifth chords flow like the ancient lava
that formed hexagonal pillars of black basalt in Fingal's Cave.
He enters it with no skiff,
just violas, cellos, and bassoons in the key of B minor.

                      *

I encountered Scotland first through Mendelssohn,
and reflect on memory of the Castle Campbell ruins,
                    lonely in a field of heather,
as I work out voicing and fingering of his arpeggiated chords.

At the piano, my mother would allow no spoken words
                          in the room.
I take it further and exclude the silent ones as well.

Elijah, Who Once Played a Violin for Stray Cats

for Elijah McClain

He lived within a body
often cold that struggled
to breathe. He built
his own boundaries,
taught himself what
he needed to know.
His hands were a gift
to skin and tissue
in need of pressure
without pain.
He played the violin
to calm stray cats
taken from streets,
and placed in cages.
He told the police:
I was just going home.
I'm an introvert.
I have no gun.
I don't do any fighting.
All I was trying to do was become better.
I'm so sorry.
I'm just different.
I just can't breathe correctly.

They pressed his carotid arteries
cut blood flow to his brain
injected him with drugs.
After that, he said nothing.
His violin is still.
Cold has taken over.

The Held Note

for Chopin

you, storyteller of the long note
count of the harmonic hours
flutterer of the sustain pedal

singer of two voices in the right hand
liberator of thumbs to play black keys
and fifth finger to find half timbre

hear a piano player in veiled clarity
small hands with supple wrists—hands
set in marble—a composer for the short life

let me play your nocturne for my own dark
let someone discover an unknown melody
that was in your mind as you lay dying

let me find the second voice each time I read you
let your held note be a candle on my way to sleep
let us be lovers in a dream

III. The Layered Life

Poem After Merwin's "One of the Lives"

because a storm called Petra has brought down heavy snow
      and I am bound by deepening drifts
I read about the last interglacial warm period newsworthy now
      because scientists on Baffin Island watching
mountain glaciers retreat backwards have found remains
      of plants that thrived more than 100,000 years ago
when sea levels were high enough to cover
      most of the settings of my life including
New York and the streets of Greenwich Village where
      I unwound the strings of youth to love unwisely
learned languages of law and poetry
      took the A train to the Cloisters to wander among
Unicorn Tapestries displaced from their European origins
      discovered that 19th century composers can heal
almost anything in me that might fracture
      and then losing the desire to live in the canyons
of tall buildings invented another life in a city with height limits
      where politics are loud and unctuous lies grate
and I must block the noise with my grand piano
      and if the violin player had not rejected my mother
and her southern belle grandmother not suggested
      it was for the best because the tall cellist chemist
would be a better husband anyway
      perhaps none of this would have happened

as I would be a different combination of genes that might not
        have chosen New York or law or piano or any city
and would embrace a more tactile field like geology
        and spend my days among rocks then
bow a stringed instrument to ease layers of tension that build
        from looking too far back or forward in time

Piano with a Mandolin Pedal

You cared for the carsick girl
who could not ride on family trips.
You played cards, checkers,

Parcheesi, as if your time were
free to spend. You sewed costumes
for Halloween, made cookies

with honey. You brushed
tangled hair gently while
telling the story of an Ohio farm

where frightful events
ended well. You played
Stephen Foster songs

about a non-existent time
on your old upright piano
with its extra mandolin

and banjo pedals until
I no longer asked for more,
and sleep had descended.

I felt safe with you until
one day you confessed to crying
but could not say why and

the Sunday you put a kitchen
knife to your throat and were taken
to the city for electroshock

therapy. Not allowed to visit,
I waved, wanly, from a sidewalk
to you behind barred windows.

Leaving

Sometimes you see things that are not
there. And sometimes you feel things
that are not real. Neither of these happens
today. The two of you wake up late
to drink black coffee mostly in silence.
You walk along the river under low clouds
attentive to boats that come, unceasingly,
one after the other. Looking only
at the river it is easy to ignore the hum
and screech of the city behind you.
So much is heavy and hovers
darkly between you, what neither
of you wants to talk about on a late
March day. Before the sun sets you
use a purloined key to enter a square
behind a locked fence, Gramercy Park,
a meditative space where talk can be
quiet and solemn, where you can speak
words that dangle in your throat,
I don't love you as I once thought I did
and *I need to leave this city before*
it swallows me with false visions,
then head alone to the brownstone
on East 18th Street, the apartment

with crumbling flowered wallpaper,
pack your clothes and notebooks,
place all your keys on the table
by the door, and close it as dark enfolds
what you have left behind.

Sacraments

Baptized Presbyterian,
I wished to be Catholic.
At seven, I stood on tiptoe
peered into the window
of Immaculate Conception
to see my other self
twirl amber rosary beads,
sign a cross head to chest
shoulder to shoulder,
confess sins on Wednesday.
At fifteen I knelt at a Wesleyan
Methodist altar, abandoned
transgressions of the flesh,
dancing, kisses, lipstick,
read the Bible twice,
planned to translate it
to a language I did not yet know.
But then I read *Exodus*,
wanted to be Jewish,
marry a bearded Semite,
adopt Diaspora history
as my own. I stopped
wearing a cross.

God became elusive.
I grew up, slept with ex-
monks and agnostics,
visited Buddhist caves,
Shinto shrines, temple ruins,
the Hagia Sophia—
Greek orthodox to mosque,
and the Great Mosque of Córdoba
with a Cathedral in its middle.

Music became my sacrament.
Verdi's Dies Irae pulses
down my spine, an electric
charge without fear.
Brahms' agnostic Requiem
blesses the living mourner,
offers release to the dead.
Mahler, Bohemian Jew
who converted Christian
to conduct in Vienna,
knew the perils of religion.
The surreal ecstasy
of his Resurrection Symphony
is the closest I come
to stepping outside
of my life.

Old Lover in a Dream

As if in a grainy Swedish film,
where actors drift in and out of roles
to confuse an unwary audience,
I am unsure now
whether I saw you last night
or only dreamed that smoky room
where you lured me to the door
with eyes that looked through
me, darkly. The decades
have not changed you, only me.
Our entanglement on Bleecker Street
lies buried, like the bones
of a small dinosaur
trapped in ice.
But your imprint on me,
like fine glacial striations
on rock, does not rub off.
Today I know again
that hot wave of nausea,
often the only warning of love.

A New York Summer: West 14th Street

The heat and grit lifted briefly.
You called to suggest coffee,
though with you it was never
just coffee. We met at the Strand,
where I searched for used
confessional poets: *Life Studies,*
For the Union Dead, Ariel,
All My Pretty Ones. I felt
less alone at the Strand,
where there was always a poet
or artist in plain view, not
pretending to be someone else.
We walked the blocks
to your neighborhood.
This was the 70s, no sidewalk cafes
with lit candles on checked table-
cloths, no spinach or kale
on the menu. We stopped at a diner
for black coffee and greasy toast.
You invited me to your walk-up
where you sketched me perched
uneasily on your blue sofa with broken
springs. My hair was long then.
You talked of the influence
of Lowell, whose heart
gave out in the back of a taxi

a few years later.
The night grew heavy.
You asked if I wanted
to lie down with you, and I did.
Tell me a story, you said,
instead of reaching for me. So
I tried to summon Scheherazade,
for whom story telling
was the art of survival.
But my mind was a blank
page in the typewriter.
I mumbled something about
my hungry cat mewling
loudly uptown in a window
by the bridge, grabbed the
confessional poets and flew

down your stairs to 14th Street,
down the subway steps
to a station deserted but for
two men who whispered
together, then pointed at me.
I bolted back up the subway steps,
up the two flights to your door
and knocked loudly—in fear
you would not open.
I thought of a story because
two men frightened me,
I muttered through tears.

That story was not good,
something about Gretel
losing her brother in the forest,
then choosing poison berries
over a house of sweet confections.
An old woman with an antidote
mysteriously appeared
so it worked out in the end,
as did the evening. We
recited lines from Keats
and slept in our clothes.
In the morning you made coffee,
offered me poems by women
I did not know and advice
for my own writing.
I regret that I was not there
the night of your first stroke,
years later. You failed
to recognize the signs—
I might have done that for you,
and told you a better story,
waiting for the medics to arrive.

In a Previous Life

I married a character in a story that was not mine.
You happened to be there when I stepped
over the girlhood boundary. Eight years
we played parts in this marriage,
but what did either of us know
of preparing a meal to accompany the wine.

In that L shaped East Village apartment,
I read Shakespeare, Tolstoy, Fitzgerald, Roth.
You played Verdi's Requiem in high volume stereo,
and the mass drew a black border around us.
New York bound us together: broken dishes,
shattered wine decanter as inevitable
as rain, summer heat wave, electrical failure.

We were cut up in car crashes in other cities.
You healed faster than me,
raged at the world more often than me.
More than one other hovered
at the edges of this story.
They seemed to be there to clarify.
When we signed papers of release,
you gave me a cut glass cat.
I still have that cat.

In the County of Dreams

An unnatural topography
where mountains circle
bodies of salted water or
slope down to flatlands of
mixed grasses, purple wildflowers.
It covers hundreds of square miles,
but the boundaries are jagged,
drawn with no deference to
what they cut.

Population density is low, and
wild animals—some almost human—
roam freely. Former lovers—
even the dead ones—show up
without warning to say things
they would never have said
outside of a dream:
> *you are not to blame for any of this.*

The deceased come alive again.
Grandmother apologizes for
attempts to end her life too soon.
Mother compliments my piano playing,
adds that my rhythm is often off.

Father still dispenses medicine
and advice and hates my politics.
My brother asks me to recite a poem
and play a nocturne.

There are strings, keyboard,
an occasional flute, percussion
that wakes me before I am ready,
before I can cross
one of those uneven borders
into another county where no one
calls my name in the dark.

House Between Willow and Maple

The house flows through me,
as I float from room to room.
No toys in the attic,
no ballet shoes or skates,
no lacy dress in a closet,
no doll left to stare unblinking
at the emptiness of a room
papered in pink flowers.
And no trace of men, father or brother.
The house speaks only of mother,
her last 30 years here alone.
She played the grand piano,
burned letters and ledgers,
wrote about childhood:

> *What a thrill to skate over the sidewalk bump*
> *at the base of our hill, and I hardly ever fell.*

Death comes down to this—
what to do with
china seldom used,
untarnished candlesticks;
what to do with a wedding ring,
a winter landscape in oils;
what to do with the fox fur
with its paws, tail, head,
and fake black button eyes.

I touch her things gingerly.
The house will sell easily.
New owners will rip off wallpaper,
build rooms reaching into the back yard.
Her spirit will be no longer welcome.
And I will not visit again—
not even to peer through glass.

Day of My Birth

Vesuvius did not explode
with the violence of year 79,
did not bury cities, mold
bodies in death, or trap
spirits in surviving walls.

It did destroy a few villages,
scarred by bombs and fascism,
26 war-weary Italians, vineyards,

all the 340th Squadron planes. Hot
ash settled to burn, melt, glaze, crack
their bodies, controls, and gun turrets.

The 340th had bombed the links
of war—bridges, tunnels, railroad
junctions. In the end, Vulcan took
more planes than enemy strikes.

An Atlantic Ocean away,
in a county where snow
coats the vernal equinox,
I had trouble navigating
the birth canal, reluctant perhaps
to enter the uncertainty—a world
populated by Nazis, bombs, volcanoes
that even after centuries do not sleep.

Meditation on Feet

So easy to take for granted
after you stop trying
to put them in your mouth,
discover they are useful
to navigate the new.
And easy to dress them—
in black patent leather, canvas,
saddle shoes, penny loafers,
sandals exposing heels and toes,
then, for a girl, high heels
that hurt with toes pointed,
rounded or squared.
I danced for years
in soft ballet slippers
until old enough to put on
the hard toe shoes I thought
would transform me into
Anna Pavlova
or Maria Tallchief,
toes wrapped in wool from
the first shearing of a lamb,
followed by the hard reality that
to dance on toes violates
some natural law of the body.
I traded the pain for a piano,
so easy on the feet,

the right up and down
on the sustain pedal,
while the left works
only once in a while
to depress the soft pedal,
moving hammers sideways
to dampen the sound,
or the sostenuto
pedal in the middle
that holds a single note
for so long as desired.
I laced my feet into boots
to hike trails with names
like Bright Angel, Cape
Final, Bristlecone Loop,
Queen's Garden, Zion
Narrows, or to wander
through broken remains
of Ephesus and Pompeii.
Eventually, they will let you down,
with their 26 bones to break
in each foot, and abundance
of nerves to pinch, compress,
burn. You can paint their nails,
to give your feet a false glamour
with colors like Amalfi Blue
or Bordeaux Red. But

in the end, all that satisfies
is to abandon shoes,
walk barefoot on sand.
The prints soon to be
obliterated.

Shell Hunt on Captiva

Angel wing, sailor's ear,
shark's eye, Venus clam,
heart cockle, crown conch,
dosinia or semele.

I walk the beach
between tidal borders,
eyes cast down
for the unbroken.

Bare feet sift fragments
of mollusk homes that rattle
like glass beads tossed
in each oncoming wave.

I envy this ability
to sweat protection
in layers of luster & symmetry,
hard curves of collectable art.

An egret watches
from surf's shallow edge,
bird and water silver in sun
cast through thin cloud cover.

I meet his wary gaze—
return to my shell game.
When I look up again,
he is gone.

Scissors

My oldest possession,
small, black, pointed,
mother's gift at five.
Grandfather objected
to the sharpness.

I cut paper hearts, snowflakes,
random asymmetrical shapes,
hair—the doll's, then my own.
Later, I cut photos of boys
who stopped calling,
stories that earned no praise.

I knew, without being told,
never to run with them,
but held them more carefully
after grandmother tried her own
on her wrists. I tested them,
gingerly, against my skin,
decided they could perhaps
inflict a lethal wound.

Though small for adult hands,
they fit my grasp well enough
I never sought another pair,
packed them for each move—

college, Manhattan,
first marriage and second,
life alone in between.

They cut flowers,
recipes I won't follow,
loose threads,
clippings on the lives
and deaths of old lovers,
the paper clutter of
thoughts unedited,
fragments of verse,
letters not sent.

I am old.
The scissors are precise,
their points still sharp.
They will cut when
I no longer can.

Consolations by Liszt Were Not Enough:
November 22, 1963

Ohio November gray,
leaves, crimson, gold,
browned and fallen.
Sophomores emerge
in winter jackets
from European history
of the year 1066
to learn that 1963
would brand them indelibly.
Wind blows into
the first stage of grief.
In the kitchens, cooks
prepare Friday night fish,
potatoes, carrots and peas,
food to be mostly
wasted that night.
The organist hurries
to the chapel to play
Bach all afternoon—
preludes, toccatas, fugues,
chorales—for those who find
calm in Baroque.
Students clump together
in warm spaces;
some cannot talk,

others cannot stop talking.
Their regular debates
on the fairness of rules—
alcohol, smoking, dress, hours—
suspended temporarily
in the darkened air.
A dorm party was planned
that night, the debate in the hall—
should it happen, should it not.
A strange compromise—
the party goes on,
the entertainment (a skit
mocking professors and deans)
does not. A party means
males can roam girls' halls, and
doors have to be propped open.
In sad defiance, I close mine.
The classical station plays
Liszt's *Consolations*,
as I numbly review
government checks and balances.
Next morning, after toast,
I pick up the exam;
my professor and I exchange
looks, each wanting to say
something, instead sighing
to say nothing.
A weekend passes, more
gray weather, a drop in degrees.

Those who watch television see
the murder of a murderer.
We stay lumped together
in our rooms, eat cold pizza,
exchange notes from missed
classes, chatter on about
Thanksgiving plans, finish
papers on Dostoyevsky and justice,
or the lack of it, trek
to a lab across campus
to look at ancient rocks,
bearing striations
of the last glacial age.
There is a long line at the casket,
a Catholic mass for the dead,
a procession to the grave
by a horse-drawn caisson.
Volumes will be written,
events replayed for anniversaries,
conspiracy theories woven,
unraveled, woven again.
The President's brain
goes missing; his sexual
affairs are exposed.
But the clop of horses' hooves
remains my most intimate
memory, the one embedded
in the hippocampus
fifty years hence.

At the Edge

Where the forest path enters a cleared field

with sheaves of hay neatly rolled, as if
they hold within remains of the summer just past,

I see two slender figures who stand too close
to be strangers. I cannot discern sex,

or whether the words they seem to be exchanging
are sharp with tension or soft with love.

They are not in the sun, but in a part of the clearing
shaded by the tall old growth

of the trees that lured me here for an afternoon. I wonder

if they belong to each other, in any sense of the word *belong*.
I do not want to come close, cause them to step aside

to let me pass or catch any words suspended between
or learn even a fragment of their story, so I turn to

a trail branch that takes a different direction.

Ice Jam

On the walk to kindergarten with my red-haired friend
the best part was Maple Street bridge where we paused
to lean over the stone railing and peer at the creek,
dry by end of summer inviting us to climb down the bank
                              and cross stone-by-stone
or frightening with its muddy waters rush in early spring thaw
or clean with snow caked on ice in a low glare of winter.

I was sorry to be home with chicken pox the day
she saw something new—two men hacking at thick ice—
and stopped to ask what they were doing;
the friendly one paused to explain that breaking ice
would prevent damming of waters and flooded
streets then he asked her name and she asked his

and at home that afternoon, still excited, she told the story
to her mother who relayed in a matter-of-fact Irish way
what was just reported on the radio—
the man who had asked her name and told her his
was swept away in a sudden surge of water
and had not yet been found.
He never was found.

I do not miss the memory that could appear
in my winter dreams—his smile and asking my name.

Norwegian Epitaph

As I pause to rest
on a graveyard bench
above a fjord, framed
this summer solstice eve
by white apple blossoms
and mountain snow
melting into water falling
over glacier carved cliffs,
an orange-striped tabby,
who seems to live
among the tombstones,
rubs against my leg
while I read the epitaph,
Tak for Alt, or
Thanks for Everything,
under the birth and death
dates of Lars, Helga, Sven,
and marvel at these Nordic spirits
who left thank you notes
as the final word.

About the Author

Carol Jennings grew up in the rolling hills of western New York, attended The College of Wooster, graduated from NYU, lived for more than a decade in New York City, and now resides in Washington DC. In New York, she worked at the United Nations and the American Civil Liberties Union before earning a J.D. from the NYU School of Law. For much of her legal career, she served in the Federal Trade Commission's Bureau of Consumer Protection. She is author of an article on "The Woman Poet," published in *The New York Quarterly* in 1972, and she served on the editorial staff of *NYQ* during the early years of its publication. Her poems have appeared in various journals, including *The New York Quarterly, Chautauqua, The Broadkill Review, Innisfree Poetry Journal, Beltway Poetry Quarterly, Oberon, Potomac Review, Medical Literary Messenger, Loch Raven Review* and *Gargoyle Magazine*, as well as three anthologies. Two of her poems have won awards at The Chautauqua Institution, where she spends time each summer. She is now retired and devotes her time to poetry and the piano.

Her first poetry collection, *The Dead Spirits at the Piano*, was published by Cherry Grove Collections in 2016.

Visit her website at: www.carol-jennings.com.

CPSIA information can be obtained
at www.ICGtesting.com
Printed in the USA
LVHW030312090723
751845LV00002B/314

9 781625 494009